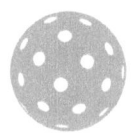

Praise For *In A Pickle*

"In A Pickle" is a game-changer for couples. I laughed, I cried! This book perfectly captures the chaos and joy of playing pickleball with your partner."

- Pickleball Pro Dave 'the Badger' Weinbach, 10-time National Champion, 15-time US Open Champion, and winner of 210 Gold Medals

"This book is dynamite for couples, blending hilarious insights with genuinely useful tips on keeping love alive while smashing it on the pickleball court. I can't recommend it enough for anyone who wants to score big in both their relationship and their pickleball game!"

- Dr. Sharon Noble, Ph.D., Couples Therapist, School Psychologist, Somatic Embodiment Coach

"In this delightful and humorous book, couples are taken on a journey of learning how to play pickleball together without driving each other crazy. The authors' witty and relatable anecdotes make this a must-read for any couple looking to strengthen their relationship while mastering a new sport."

- Kevin Beeson, KB Pickleball, Senior Pro Player, 3-time National Champion, Touring Teaching Professional, and Author of *Pickleball Metaphors: The Fast Track to Better Pickleball*

"This book is a delightful blend of beauty and humor. By reading it, not only will you enhance your game, but you will also strengthen your connection with your better half on the court. Enjoy the journey!"

- Fernanda Aragon, Pickleball Pro, COPA LATAM PICKLEBALL National Women's Doubles Champion for Costa Rica

"A must-read for any pickleball-playing couple. It's a hilarious and insightful look at the challenges and rewards of playing with your spouse."

- Tim Klitch, Founder & Chief Fun Officer at Austin Pickle Ranch and General Manager and part-owner of Major League Pickleball's Texas Ranchers

IN A PICKLE

How to Master Love and Pickleball
and Not Kill Each Other

DR. STORMY HILL
AND
TERI CITTERMAN

Foreword by Dr. Joel Bell, Ph.D., LMHC, son of
pickleball co-inventor Bill Bell

IN A PICKLE: How to Master Love and Pickleball and Not Kill Each Other

Copyright ©2024 by Stormy Hill and Teri Citterman

All rights reserved. No part of this book may be reproduced in any manner whatsoever without the expressed written permission of the author.

Glisan Muir
PRESS

Published by Glisan Muir Press

Paperback ISBN: 979-8-9915194-1-0
Hardback ISBN: 979-8-9915194-0-3
ePub ISBN: 979-8-9915194-2-7

Every attempt has been made to properly source all quotes and attribute all research.

Printed in the United States of America

First Edition

IN A PICKLE

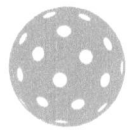

Dedication

To Steve Johnson and Pradeep (Raj) Rajurs

Without you, we would never have learned the highs and the lows of navigating the court with the men we love. Thank you for the countless hours of encouragement and support, play on the court, and dialogue about the book. We are forever grateful and elevated as pickleball players and humans.

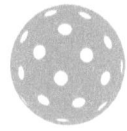

Table of Contents

Foreword	11
Message to the Reader	15
Introduction	19
Chapter 1: The First Rule of Pickleball	25
Chapter 2: No One Thinks They're a Bad Communicator	33
Chapter 3: Feedback Finesse	47
Chapter 4: Playing with Intention vs. "In Tension"	61
Chapter 5: Navigating Conflict on the Court	69
Chapter 6: How to Elevate Your Pickleball EQ	85
Chapter 7: Your Pickleball Love Language	99
Chapter 8: A Banger and a Dinker Walk Into a Bar	111
Chapter 9: Safe Words and Other Success Strategies	121
Conclusion: Mastering Love and Pickleball	135
Glossary	139
Acknowledgments	141
About the Authors	143

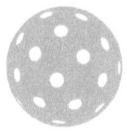

Foreword

I have literally grown up with pickleball because my dad, Bill Bell, along with my godfather, Joel Pritchard, invented the game one afternoon in the summer of 1965.

You are probably familiar with pickleball's distinctive charm. You know how it's easy to play and uncomplicated to learn. Part of pickleball's appeal is that you can accelerate any rally into a rapid game of strategy, and the game scales to whatever degree of athleticism you bring to it.

The origin story is often speculated, but here is the real deal. The Bells and the Pritchards were spending the summer on Bainbridge Island, WA, a short ferry ride from Seattle. Frank Pritchard, then 14 years old, was bored. He wanted to be back in Seattle with his pals.

"When I was young, we used to make up games," said my uncle Joel.

"Oh yeah?" sulked Frank. "So, make up a game, then."

My dad and Joel discovered that a discarded wiffle ball bounced true on the old badminton court, and with the net lowered, they improvised a kind of mini-tennis with ragged, wooden paddles. "There you go kids, a game."

But we kids were crowded out pretty quickly, as our folks and their friends took over the court. There weren't many racket sports one could play with a paddle in one hand and a cocktail in the other, while arguing politics, and making it up as you go.

The whole spirit of the game was like a hand-me-down. The serve was underhanded and diagonal like tennis. The scoring, with the server, was like ping pong, and play was to 11 or 21 points like volleyball. Eventually, the "No-Volley Zone" acquired a better designation as "The Kitchen," borrowed from shuffleboard, probably the laziest game ever devised.

Left out of pickleball's origin story is the fact that my dad was a spy, which enlightens a few things. Dad's influence on the game, like his double life, helps explain how pickleball is actually a game of strategy more than athleticism.

And rightly so, Teri and Stormy have packed this book full of strategies from communication and feedback to safe words and psychological warfare. I think my dad would have loved it.

The amalgam of rules grafted from other sports is what led to its name. Joel's wife, Joan Pritchard, coined the game pickleball because it reminded her of her rowing crew in college. Rowers who failed to make either the "A" or "B" boat were relegated to the "Pickle Boat." All the left-overs fell in there, and pickleball was certainly a game of leftovers.

And, to put it to rest, the game was not named for Pickles, the Pritchards' dog.

Originally social, not competitive, pickleball has evolved into an intense sport. Couples who gathered to play in a backyard, driveway, or repurposed tennis court rarely left them headed for divorce court.

But, things change. My family's game is now the occasion for all levels of frustration and competitive angst that it never intended to create. Couples may be seeking a fun activity, but when one spouse is a little or a lot more competitive, a day of fun turns into frustration. Thus, the reason this book is so important.

Pickleball's pace, rituals, and sociability permit me to manage my own competitive streak. I'm a smack talker. During the game, I distract, frustrate, and annoy my opponent via relentless banter. Ask my wife - I definitely could have used this book.

As a therapist and psychologist, I've never mediated a pickleball-induced marital crisis, but doubles games have a knack for amplifying hidden issues. We've all met that nice couple who turn nasty when the game heats up, right? *In A Pickle* offers a clever approach for couples to navigate these challenges on the court.

Teri and Stormy share personal stories of frustrations (and growth) while playing with their spouses, allowing readers to see themselves in the variety of personalities reflected. Teri's direct, CEO-advising style complements Stormy's therapy-based approach to enhancing communication between partners. We also meet Raj and Steve, who bring their own strengths and quirks to the book and the court.

In A Pickle is quick and fun to read, rich with actual advice that takes practice to master, just like the game itself.

Enjoy!

- Dr. Joel Bell, Ph.D., LMHC,
Therapist and Author of
5 Star Trust: A Memoir About Bill Bell

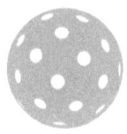

Message to the Reader

When you play pickleball with your spouse and the two of you are in sync, there is no better feeling. There is trust. There is rhythm. It's as if you're an extension of the other – shakin' and bakin' and dominating the court.

Everyone wants more of that!

This book is for anyone who wants to play pickleball with their intimate partner whether in same-sex or different-sex relationships.

Intended Benefits

You know the adage, 'what doesn't kill you makes you stronger'? In pickleball, there are no truer words spoken. Pickleball will uncover what you never even knew irked you about your spouse. And the feelings will be mutual.

Yes, there will be moments of laughter and joy, but as you and your spouse improve and the tentacles of competition creep in, we've seen the rising tension outweigh the lightheartedness. Like any sport, the game is designed to bring out your competitive nature, and if you or your spouse are innately competitive, then this book is for you.

We've packed it full of lessons learned, stories we've heard and strategies to improve your mixed doubles game. It's designed to help you play better, love more, and win more points. Our hope is your relationship will be more fun and fulfilling, your game up-leveled, and no one will end up on an episode of Dateline.

Cautionary Warning

And just like having a baby, if your relationship is on a downward trajectory, taking up pickleball as a last resort "fun thing to do together" is a terrible idea. Pickleball will not save your marriage. In fact, it will ignite the last bits of anything worth saving into a burning inferno of sadness, disappointment, and blame.

MESSAGE TO THE READER

Court Chemistry: How Well Do You Know Your Partner?

This is the first of many exercises to do together if you really want to elevate your game as a couple. Answer for each other and see which responses you get right! Bonus points if you capture your couple interviews on video and send it to us!

1. What would be your partner's "enter the court" theme song?
2. What's your partner's signature move on the pickleball court?
3. What's your partner's most annoying habit on the court?
4. What's your partner's best shot? Worst shot?
5. Who is better at keeping track of the score?
6. If you had team uniforms, what colors would they be?
7. What's the best way to celebrate victory after the match?

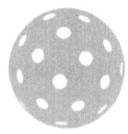

Introduction

Stepping onto the pickleball court with my partner, I'm suddenly flooded with a barrage of thoughts:

Move your feet. Stay back on serve. Return and run. Cover the middle. Drive hard, but not too hard. Dink soft, but not too soft. And no matter what, don't pop it up.

Then my partner says,
"Just have fun, babe. Don't overthink it. . ."

Are you f*ck!ng kidding me?!

How can this silly sport on this tiny court be so overwhelming, intriguing, addicting, and infuriating all at once? Welcome to the world of pickleball - a microcosm of your relationship.

The Pickleball Phenomenon

Pickleball is the fastest-growing sport in America, with millions of new players picking up a paddle every day. It induces an unexplainable allegiance, a cult disguised as a casual pastime. The addictive combination of competition and community has converted countless innocents. It's also one of the only sports where mixed doubles is as popular as same-gender doubles.

As droves of couples storm the courts with the intention of having fun together, they're coming face to face with a lethal combination of conflict, criticism, and competition with their spouse. It's no wonder both marriage counseling and divorce are on the rise. Coincidence? We doubt it.

The Double-Edged Paddle

Navigating the pickleball court with your spouse as your teammate is full of opportunities (ha!). You can either rock it as a relational unit or rip each other apart like rabid hyenas. When things get competitive, the pressure becomes immense.

William Shakespeare coined the term "in a pickle" to denote a challenging and tense situation under pressure. While relationships are full of "pickles," one place couples can deeply feel this intensity is on the pickleball court.

At the same time, there are choices we make on the court. How you choose to treat, communicate, and support each other is

INTRODUCTION

fundamental to a successful pickleball partnership and life together.

Reader Dedication

This book is for pickleball-playing couples who love the idea of playing together but don't love what happens when eye rolls and irritation take over the court. Our main goal is to show you how it doesn't have to be this way. You can master the court with your spouse and continue to enjoy and excel at this sport we all love.

About the Authors

Stormy Hill is a mental health therapist and relationship coach from Salt Lake City, where you can ski some of the best peaks and play pickleball all in the same day.

Teri Citterman is an executive coach from Seattle, the birthplace of pickleball, who now resides in Austin, Texas, home to some of the top pro pickleball players in the world.

We are doubles partners at the 3.5 - 4.0 level. We met in Costa Rica and found we shared a love for pickleball and for our respective partners. Sometimes, the combination of the two ignites a chemical explosion that teeters on the edge of amazement, before it plummets into a cesspool of disappointment.

We've experienced the pickleball highs and lows with our partners. Some days we are the couple to be reckoned with. Other days, our looks can kill, words can wound, and it's not just us.

We've witnessed this dynamic between couples at rec play, drill practice, and at camps, clinics, and tournaments. Husbands, wives, spouses, significant others, life partners, soulmates, and lovers are in conflict and losing points and faith in each other because of it.

We know the anguish and the addiction firsthand.

Why We Wrote This Book

Admittedly, there have been times on the court when we've behaved badly - pissy and mean, to be exact. And yes, there are words we can never unsay. But we have also been the recipients of such behavior, which sucks at the very least, and puts the entire relationship in question if you're not careful.

Many people don't just want to play pickleball for fun. They want to partner with their spouse, play well, and win. That's what inspired us to write this book. As avid pickleball players and competitive women, we want to play with our significant others and be powerhouse couples on and off the court.

When you spend an inordinate amount of time living your addiction to this sport and playing with the person you're sleeping with, there are bound to be big highs and even bigger lows.

And let's be honest, as amazing as this sport is, it is the root cause for what we call "kitchen knife moments" - those times when you think you want to kill your partner or at least whack them really hard with your paddle.

INTRODUCTION

Our hope is that by using the strategies in this book, those moments become less frequent and your pickleball playing becomes a bridge to more fun, more connection, and more wins.

Good luck and happy dinking!

1
The First Rule of Pickleball

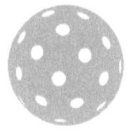

The First Rule of Pickleball

The first rule of pickleball? Don't be a dick.

The second rule of pickleball? Don't be a dick.

Like in Vegas, what happens on the pickleball court stays on the pickleball court. (Ha, hardly!) If it were only that simple. The reality is pickleball is a mirror. Like any sport, it reflects your highest highs during the thrill of victory – and your lowest lows in the agony of defeat. Throw in relationship dynamics between you and your partner, and every moment becomes a master class in self-control.

You can have a solid, supportive relationship in real life, but humans are messy. Some days, when you step onto the court and the ball is served, it's as if something takes over your body, mind, and mouth – and brings out your inner asshole.

Thus, the need for the first rule of pickleball.

And because anyone who says "it goes without saying" knows it must be said. Everyone has it in them to be a dick. We use this as a non-endearing, genderless term that can either be in reference to the reader of this book or their spouse.

When the heat turns up, thick skin becomes thin, eye rolls become audible, and whispered words stab like a knife.

Exaggeration? Maybe. But you know what we mean. As unfortunate as it is, there will come a time on the court when the love of your life, your pickleball teammate, becomes the person you most want to annihilate. Presume the feeling is mutual.

If only the two of you could harness that energy to beat your opponent. Instead, you use it to beat each other by slinging angry words and airing deep-rooted frustration to lose the point, if not the game. Your opponents win by no action of their own – by letting a simple divide and conquer strategy play out.

When (not if) this happens, know it's not an opinion. You know when you're being a dick and so does everyone else. It's a fact. Take heed of the advice Teri gave her stepson during his formative years: "Just try harder not to be one."

Rules Saved Our Game
Sarah & Dave

Dave and I have been married for over a decade, and we're inseparable in most aspects of our lives. But when it comes to pickleball, our partnership has been a rollercoaster.

At first, the court was a battleground. Dave's competitive spirit would clash with my more laid-back approach. "You're hitting too low!" he'd shout. "I'm trying to volley!" I'd retort.

One evening, after a particularly fiery match, we sat down for a much-needed beer. "We need to figure this out," I said. "We're supposed to be a team."

Besides the rule: Don't be a dick, we decided to create a set of rules to make our pickleball partnership more enjoyable:

- No yelling or arguing. If we disagree, we'll discuss it calmly after the match.

- Focus on having fun. The goal isn't just to win, but to enjoy spending time together.
- Encourage each other. Celebrate each other's successes and offer support during tough moments.

Following these rules transformed our pickleball partnership. We started cheering each other on, laughing at our mistakes, and even helping each other improve. Our love for the game grew, as did our love for each other.

- Sarah

KEY TAKEAWAYS

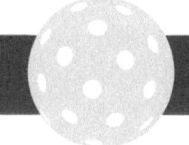

Pickleball Points

- Pickleball can be a serious relationship stress test. Figure out how to keep it fun.

- You know each other better than anyone. Use that to your advantage by keeping your cool.

- Anyone can be a dick. Try hard not to be one.

Court Chemistry

- ♥ When the competition starts to rise, what's the one thing each of you can do to avoid being a dick to your partner?

2

No One Thinks They're a Bad Communicator

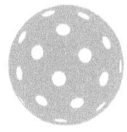

No One Thinks They're a Bad Communicator

For centuries, psychiatrists, anthropologists, and criminal investigators have tried to uncover the nuance of communication between partners. But in pickleball, it's far simpler. The real power in a relationship is when your partner sets you up for a killer shot and screams those three prized words:

"PUT! IT! AWAY!"

Communication is an art and a skill that can be practiced and improved. When you're good at it, you can avoid most misunderstandings, which are the source of 80% of conflict.

The Bad News

On the small size of the pickleball court, all your communication faux pas are illuminated. The drama becomes Drama with a capital D, and the punishment outweighs the crime. Sometimes the court feels like a cage, and you are in it with either your best friend or your mortal enemy. It all depends on how well the game is going.

The Better News

Maybe instead of a cage, it's a stage where you and your partner can both improve your communication. If you do, your game will get better too. Unforced errors will decrease, points will increase, and you will experience a new level of relationship joy where you get to win together.

Healthy vs. Unhealthy Communication

As a relationship coach, Dr. Stormy has seen countless couples taken down by poor communication. It is the reason for almost every struggle in a relationship. The same applies to the pickleball court.

Sharing an activity fosters understanding and support for one another. How cool is it when you and your spouse are each other's greatest cheerleaders? Playing this sport requires a high level of trust. You trust them to do their job and they trust you. When you have that on the court, it translates into life.

Healthy Communication is Key

Where do you recognize yourself and your significant other? By the way, this is (another) good exercise to do together.

» Active listening: Listening with your full attention during the venting they need to do after the game.

» Open body language: During and after the games, keep an open stance with uncrossed arms to avoid shutting out your partner.

» Eye contact: Make eye contact to foster intimacy and trust. Try not to look away in disgust when your partner hits the game point into the net. Instead give them a loving look because it sucked for them too.

» "I" statements: Using "I" instead of "you" minimizes blame and lessens defensiveness. "I didn't play well today and we could improve how we move as a team" goes further than "What the hell were you doing! Why can't you just stay with me on the court?"

» Acknowledge mistakes: Be willing to acknowledge when you're wrong and apologize. "Sorry baby, I was a jerk today" is a wonderful way to reset and get back to loving.

It would be impressive if we were strong enough, confident enough, and nice enough to always make healthy communication choices. But sometimes we fly too close to the sun. We let loose an impulsive, thoughtless remark and are surprised when our partner storms off the court.

Then there's communication that triggers volcanic reactions. Which of these strike a nerve? Once you know where you struggle, you can figure out how to course correct.

Unhealthy Communication is Toxic

- » Being a poor listener and ignoring your partner's ball calls or helpful insight.
- » Being aggressive by attacking or criticizing on the court.
- » Being passive-aggressive (saying yes when you mean no). Smiling while seething with rage inside.
- » Interrupting your partner's line calls, feedback, and just anything they try to say.
- » Blaming them for out balls, bad shots, and lost games.
- » Being defensive at the smallest piece of advice your partner shares.

What's Your Communication Style?

You and your partner are a unit in life and on the court, but you're still individuals with particular preferences. How you communicate off the court is exactly the same as on the court.

Which of these communication styles do you and your partner most identify with?

1. Give me the facts quickly. Let's decide and move on – short and direct.
2. Let's share a laugh and ease into the conversation – softer and slower.
3. Let me hear your side and then I'll share mine – collaborative and connecting.
4. Give me all the details and then let me go think about it – information and then processing.

While you can't change how your partner communicates, you can learn to communicate together in a way that works for your relationship.

For example, when Teri met Raj, he was extremely passive aggressive (his words, not hers). He said yes when he meant no. He'd say nothing was wrong, but inside he was fuming. He was naturally conflict averse, until he wasn't. Then, he would explode. By the way, his repressed anger eventually led to all kinds of health issues, but that's another story for another book.

On the other hand, there's nothing passive about Teri's aggressiveness. She is no-bullshit direct. What you see is what you get. They are different, and it works for them. Since they've been together, Teri claims she's gotten nicer and Raj has become more assertive.

Stormy and Steve are just the opposite on and off the pickleball court. Stormy is soft, kind, and verbose. Steve talks when he has something to say, but otherwise is happily quiet. Stormy loves to emote, and Steve is more of a closed book. Since they've been together, Stormy claims she's gotten more direct, and Steve has become more emotive.

Communicate in the best way your partner can hear you. What's hard about that!?!

Communication Starts With . . . Communication

If you think about it, you likely know how your spouse prefers to be communicated with. For example, maybe it's direct, or maybe it's a softer approach. If you don't know how your partner likes to receive communication - ask them.

Consider the pickleball court your living, breathing, communication workshop.

We know a married couple who play pickleball together. He is positive, gentle, and kind. She is sensitive and very direct. When she tells him to "fix that shit," he does exactly that. She knows what she means, and he knows what she means. It works for them. Their communication up-levels their pickleball game and seems to work perfectly in their lives. They've been married 30 years and are one of the happiest and strongest couples we know.

Something to aspire to!

The very first time Stormy played pickleball with Steve, within the first 30 seconds, he made the mistake of criticizing every shot. She was literally trying to figure out the crazy scoring, get her serves to stay in the court, and keep the ball in play. His visible irritation and firehose of feedback did not help. In fact, it made her play worse and pissed her off, which is not easy to do. Finally, she stopped mid-point and declared "THAT sort of communication is NOT going to work for me!"

Needless to say, that first 30 minutes was the beginning of a long journey to learning how to communicate and play together as a team. Just like any couple, some days are still better than others.

So while communication styles may vary, poor communication or non-communication (yes it is a form of communication) is at the root of almost every argument. Non-communication can be: avoiding eye contact, rejecting your partner's offer for a "boop" (paddle tap after a point), or walking away in a huff. Non-communication is an avoidance strategy.

In fact, Teri used to say if Raj competed in a speech contest using only body language, he would've won. His acerbic sighs were deafeningly, leaving no doubt about his thoughts, yet he was oblivious to how his silent outbursts affected others, especially his targets.

Teri wasted no time confronting Raj, forcing him to realize the impact of his non-verbal actions. Like words can't be unsaid, eye rolls can't be taken back. This has made him question why he feels compelled to react so judgmentally. Is it a need to be right? Or to be perfect? Or both?

Pickleball is a silly game and a glaring metaphor for many marital struggles. Despite his competitive nature, Raj consciously prioritized his marriage. He works hard to be less reactive and judgmental on the court, and in their relationship.

Practice your communication and you will win more points, enjoy the game, and appreciate each other. Lives get busy. Playing pickleball is a massive injection of fun. The goal is to have more laughter and fewer kitchen knife moments, because in the end, it's just pickleball.

Communication Do's

» **Over Communicate** - Keep it simple. Call the ball. A perfect game would sound like both of you yelling: "MINE!" "MINE!" "MINE!" It may be annoying, but calling your shots is a great way to improve your communication and your game.

- **YOURS!** - Theoretically, you're only supposed to call MINE, not YOURS. But let's be real. If I ain't getting the ball, even if it looks like it's mine to get, I'm calling YOURS!

- **Who's Got the Middle!?!** - Pickleball pro Dave "the Badger" Weinbach etched it into our brains during one of his pickleball camps. It's become a "rallying cry" for anyone who's playing together and misses the shot that comes right down the middle. Note: There are two recommended strategies. Raj and Teri play the "forehand player covers the middle." Stormy and Steve play "respect the X[1]." Just decide on your strategy and stick to it.

- **Out. Leave!** - Balls hit hard that are whizzing by your shoulders are really juicy and irresistible, but they are easy points, if you can let them go out. When you see your partner winding up, call it out!

- **Switch!** Call "switch" when you poach or cover a lob on your partner's side (otherwise it's confusing) and "stay." It's switch and stay.

- **Affirmations** - Sprinkle in plenty of "nice shot!" and "great get!" affirmations throughout the game. The human

---

1. Respect the X is a concept that involves handling cross-court shots that cross over an X formation made by two players who are diagonal from each other. The player on the other end of the line should generally handle these shots.

brain craves positive reinforcement. Make a conscious effort to dish out encouragement more than anything.

Communication Don'ts

» **Negativity** - Saying things that are critical or picking on your spouse is a sure way to lose points. People rarely respond well to negative comments. Why bother wasting your breath and making things worse for the person who's clearly struggling?

» **Mid-point Commands** - Yelling commands during a point that causes your partner to tense up and get flustered . . . not helpful.

» **Blame and Shame!** - Do you really want to make your partner feel bad? That's the only thing that results from blame or shame. Unless you never ever make an error, best to think this one through.

» **Non-verbal** - Not all communication is verbal. Heavy sighs and dirty looks communicate loudly.

» **Sweep it Under the Rug** - This passive strategy only leads to resentment and a very bumpy rug, so to speak.

KEY TAKEAWAYS

Pickleball Points

- The quality of your communication directly impacts the outcome of the game.
- Know thyself, know thy partner. Communication styles matter.
- Be each other's MVP. Support and encouragement wins championships.

Court Chemistry

- Plan ahead. What would be the perfect thing for your partner to say or do when you hit the game point sailing into the net? What do they want you to say (or not say) when the same thing happens to them?

3
Feedback Finesse

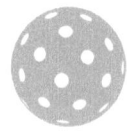

Feedback Finesse

If that's the sound of your eyes rolling, your feedback is not helpful. However, receiving constructive feedback is critical, if you want to get better at anything. Whether it's developing a stronger relationship or improving in pickleball, learning how to give and take is key. Our most valuable piece of feedback…?

Remember the first rule of pickleball: Don't be a dick.

Taking on the challenge of learning new skills together not only bolsters individual confidence, but also strengthens the bond between partners. As an added bonus, this shared growth is a fantastic workout for the brain, promoting cognitive health and resilience.

Getting feedback is one of the fastest ways to improve your game. But feedback between spouses is tricky. Stormy saw a t-shirt that read, "If I am not paying you for your feedback, then I don't want it." Yep, that's the truth. Getting unsolicited advice, especially from your partner, even if they're a 4.5 or better player, is challenging.

> *I can tell Stormy 100 times what to do to improve her game, but when a pro tells her, she listens.*
>
> *- Steve*

However, feedback (both the positive kind and the opportunity kind, which most people call negative) is important if you actually want to improve your game. Sometimes you already know what you did wrong or why that ball went straight into the net. But occasionally, your partner sees something you didn't or has a quick tip to change the outcome of your ball going into the net again.

Yet we rarely see couples exchanging feedback effectively. Usually, in a heartbeat, the game goes off the rails. Watch the next time this happens with you and your spouse. More than likely you will lose the next point or two or ten. When you're in tension, you've just handed the game to your opponents.

The 3 T's of Feedback

If feedback is so valuable, how do you navigate this precarious dance of giving and receiving it? We like the 3T's approach. This is a strategy Stormy adopted from a popular sex coach, Dr. Emily Morse, and she uses it with almost all the couples she coaches on having difficult and important conversations. Since we know the satisfaction of a hard put-away rivals a great orgasm, we figured this strategy aptly applies.

3 T's

Timing: *When?*

Tone: *How?*

Turf: *Where?*

The 3 T's are Timing, Tone, and Turf.

Timing: Consider the timing of your feedback. Timing is everything. During a point is NOT the time to offer your brilliance on what your partner can do better. It will only piss your partner off, causing them to tense up, grip the paddle tighter, and sail the ball out or into the net - probably in that order. A safer choice would be after the point or when the game is over.

But even then, blurting it out is risky. Why not simply ask your partner, "Are you open to some feedback?" That way, he, she or they gets to decide if they are in a space to hear what you have to say. If they are, great. Permission granted. If they say no, bite your tongue . . . harder!

Tone: The concept "men are from Mars, women are from Venus" becomes glaringly apparent on the pickleball court. Making some broad stroke assumptions, it can be said that men learn through challenge and women learn through praise. Consider that when you're offering feedback. If you want your significant other to listen, then say it in a way they can hear it. That achieves both the goal of giving it and it being received.

Stormy and her partner were playing rec play and the vibe was off. It was a hot, muggy day in Costa Rica, and they were both a touch hungover. Stormy's boyfriend was giving her what seemed to be endless feedback, and she was not open to hearing it. Suddenly, in exasperation, he gave her a directive, "That was yours! Cover the middle. Understood!?"

"WHAT?! Go fuck yourself. How's that for understanding!"

Needless to say the next point did not go well and neither did the rest of the game. Although they both laugh about it now, at the moment, it was not funny.

Turf: If you take nothing else from this book, let it be this: The court is a sensitive place. For some, receiving feedback on the court is the perfect place. How else would you make the necessary adjustments to win the game? For most others, the court is, or at least should be, a feedback-free zone.

If you've agreed to exchange feedback in the moment, then good on ya. Go crazy! Immediate feedback does make the most sense. But read the room. If your partner is struggling in their play or not open, then your feedback is going to land like a rock, and you'll find yourself in a hard place. It may be better to hold off until the car ride home. Or after a glass of wine. Or maybe never.

Positive > Negative

The other key thing about feedback is that it needs to be BOTH kinds of feedback – positive and opportunity. Yes, "opportunity" sounds a little like "everyone gets a trophy," but that's not exactly it. It's more about choosing to showcase the opportunity for improving without being negative.

But it's astounding how easily negative feedback slides off the tongue. Think about the last time you tried giving your spouse feedback on how to load the dishwasher. It probably started out innocently enough, but quickly disintegrated into a puddle of obscenities.

Here's the deal. No one is motivated by hearing what they do wrong. And when the giver is caught in the groove of negativity, they are poised for a well-deserved kitchen knife moment on the pickleball court or, God forbid, in the actual kitchen where the real knives are kept.

We mentioned that women often learn through praise, and positive feedback is a great form of praise. The human brain tracks negativity and internalizes it more deeply (an old survival tactic dating back to caveman days). So the best thing to do is keep things balanced by offering equal parts opportunity and positivity.

Surely, your partner did something right in the game. They probably hit some good shots, even a great shot or two. It may feel challenging, but if you acknowledge the good, your partner will be more interested in hearing what you have to say when it's not good.

> **If the right words escape you, here are a few ideas:**
>
> "great shot"
>
> "great poach"
>
> "you're amazing"
>
> "so close"
>
> "right idea"

Most people play better with partners who are positive or at least neutral. "I love my very negative partner," said no one ever! Not to mention, negativity is a complete turn off. Seriously!

Two-Way Street

Like nearly all things in a relationship, feedback is a two-way street. At least, it's supposed to be.

There is a certain persona who believes they know everything and are just being helpful. Similar to dishing negative feedback, for them, feedback, in general, slides out of their mouths as if it's slathered in fish oil. But they don't necessarily welcome feedback in return. Why would they need it?

If only one person is on the receiving end most of the time, then that game you're playing is extra-sucky for them. Don't expect to just offer your "brilliant" insights without being open to receiving your spouse's observations in return.

Now with couples, it's likely one of you is a more skilled player, which means you may have more advice to help your partner improve. One of you might be more of a strategist (maybe you play tennis) and know how to read the court. That's a great advantage against opponents and a learning opportunity for your partner.

For Teri and Raj, part of the challenge of playing together is that Raj is a natural athlete. He was a cricket champion, a tennis champion, and a scratch golfer within a short time of picking up a club. His inherent desire to be the best translated into a scientific study of the game, coupled with the engineering precision needed to master it.

But most people are not like that. While Teri excels in physical activities like dance and trapeze, she knew if she wanted to play doubles with Raj, and avoid his sharp criticism masked as feedback, she'd need to up her game.

Raj knew that too, so he encouraged Teri to take lessons from various pros. In fact, as an anniversary present, Raj gifted her a week of pickleball camp in Costa Rica. The feedback was pointed, but less charged so Teri was open to hearing and incorporating it. That is a gift they both benefit from.

The bottom line is, the value of feedback is priceless. It's the delivery that can be soul crushing. Send a little love when you're delivering it, and on the receiving end, thicken up your skin. Not everything is personal, even though it may feel like it. Or, take a word of warning from Raj. When the feedback trough is full and your partner's blood is beginning to boil, Raj tells Teri to "video yourself." That way, you can see what you need to improve on your own, and your partner can keep their mouth shut.

Feedback Do's

» Ask "Are you open to feedback?" This allows your partner to decide whether they are open or not to your insights.

» Be open to both giving AND receiving feedback. It is likely that you can see all your spouse's mistakes AND they can see yours. So remember feedback is a two-way street.

» Sometimes "staying in your own lane" is the best approach. Feedback is not always needed and it is best received when given kindly and thoughtfully. And sometimes the best approach is just trusting that your spouse can see their own mistakes just as you can see yours.

» Avoid giving feedback during a point or shot.

» Consider the way in which you are giving feedback. Could it be more kind? A little more graceful? Are you being a dick?

» When drilling or when playing and both parties agree that they are open to feedback, then it makes sense to stop after the point to analyze or instruct.

Feedback Don'ts

- Offer unsolicited feedback.
- Offer feedback when your partner has asked you not to.
- Offer only negative feedback.
- Happily offer feedback but be unwilling to receive it.
- Blame your partner for their errors.
- Bring the angst from the court home with you. Leave it on the court as best as you can.

KEY TAKEAWAYS

Pickleball Points

- Timing matters. Don't unload your thoughts mid-match. Pick your moment wisely.//
- Listen more, talk less. Hear your partner out before chiming in or getting defensive.
- Be a cheerleader, not a coach. Everyone loves a little praise. Mix it with constructive feedback for a winning combo.
- Don't dink around. Be honest, not hurtful. Improve your game, not your grudge.

Court Chemistry

- What are specific ways you can create a safe space for both of you to share your feelings and ideas without feeling defensive or attacked?
- How can you make sure your feedback is about the game, and not the person?

4

Playing with Intention vs. "In Tension"

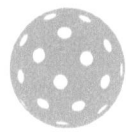

Playing with Intention vs. "In Tension"

The line between deciding your intention and finding yourself in tension is narrow. On the way to the club, you and your spouse are a confident couple, unstoppable, poised for victory. But from the first serve on, confidence turns to confusion, "Who's got the middle?"[2] becomes WTF! and you find yourselves furiously in tension and seething with rage.

What the hell just happened?

---

2. A "rally cry" by Dave "the Badger" Weinbach, when your opponent hits the ball straight down the middle and creates confusion between partners.

Three powerful strategies to help shift you from tension to cohesion are intentions, goal setting, and gratitude. These proven tools help people be more successful in life, love, and pickleball.

Power of Intention

Nothing beats being in the zone with your partner. When you and your spouse are setting each other up for the put-aways, trusting that you've got the middle, knowing you both have each other's backs, you are winning! This is what happens when you are playing with intention, rather than playing in tension.

Setting an intention is not some woo-woo, hippie way of hoping for the best. It is a well-studied strategy to direct your thoughts, actions, and energy. Typically, an intention is a commitment to yourself that is aligned with action. It can be one word or a few words that you invoke to help you stay focused.

> **Examples of Setting Intention:**
>
> Have fun today.
>
> Move my feet. Run for the ball.
>
> Drop my third shots.
>
> One more ball in play.
>
> Move with my partner.
>
> Serve strong. Stay focused.

PLAYING WITH INTENTION VS. "IN TENSION"

Slow down.

Play competitive.

Bring the energy.

You see how varied intentions can be. That's why it is good to set your intention each day that you head to the court. It's also a great practice for both you and your spouse to set an intention, then share them with each other. That way, from the start you can know whether you're aligned.

If your intention is "playing a chill game" and your partner's is "to win at any cost," then your intentions are misaligned. In fact, your whole approach may be misaligned and that's important to recognize.

Teri's competitive nature is well-known, but is not the same as her husband's. Raj mentioned this one day, which surprised her. "You like to compete, but you're not ultra-competitive," he replied. Teri bristled.

When winning is paramount, Raj will reach deep into his reserves to pull out the skill necessary to win. If he loses, he'll fight to the end. That's how intention quickly moves to being in tension. If Teri loses, she doesn't dwell on it. Raj, with his perfectionism, does. Raj acknowledges people are different, and so to play together, his intention is to occasionally check his ultra-competitiveness and remember it's a choice to play with Teri.

Getting clarity on each other's intentions is a good conversation to have before you step onto the court.

During a day of play, Stormy's intention was power. Steve's intention was finesse. This worked well for them. While she worked on her power game, he handled the drops and the resets. They were in flow with their intentions and won most of their points.

Conversely, when Stormy's intention was to "just have fun" and Steve's intention was to "crush the opponents," one might imagine what it looks like to put a fire out by pouring gasoline on it. Not pretty, and also ineffective.

Steve and Stormy were in tension. While Stormy was offering smiley faced "good tries" and laughing at her errors, Steve's blood pressure was rising. He sneered at each missed shot, including his own, and poached 90% of the court. They were on the struggle bus, and there were no more stops on the route. Recognizing they were in tension made it easier not to say something they couldn't take back. That is a serious demonstration of self control, folks.

Goal Setting

When you set a goal, it makes it six times more likely you will meet it. Goal setting has been studied by science and change theorists for a long time. It's a powerful strategy for success in every setting from corporate America to personal development to professional athletes, and it applies to relationships and to the pickleball court.

Why? Because our brain likes a challenge. When we set a goal, our brain immediately kicks into action toward achieving that goal. That's what it takes to change.

Goal → Action → Change

When Stormy and Steve set a goal and defined the actions, it was game changing.

Knowing each other's goals is a smart way to support each other. When working toward your goals, you will automatically have more grace with yourself and with your spouse, when they make errors. Because after all, achieving a goal is about making mistakes, learning from them, and mastering the shots you practice.

Gratitude Goes A Long Way

We won't bore you with the myriad of ways that gratitude can improve your life, your happiness, and your mental health. Though it does! Gratitude shifts our mindset in ways few other things do. And a positive mindset, when playing pickleball with your partner, is more than half the battle.

If we take a step back, pickleball provides a wealth of things to be thankful for. Our ability to run, jump, and compete on the court. The sheer exhilaration and happiness the game brings us. The camaraderie we share with our pickleball partners and opponents. The satisfaction of seeing our skills improve with each match played. Lean into gratitude because you get to play this sport with your lover.

KEY TAKEAWAYS

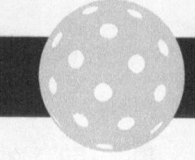

Pickleball Points

- Mind over matter. Your thoughts shape your game.
- Gratitude is your secret weapon. Focus on the positive.
- Goals fuel success. Set them, achieve them, repeat.

Court Chemistry

- ♥ What keeps each of you from staying focused on the court, and what do each of you need to do to minimize distraction?

5

Navigating Conflict on the Court

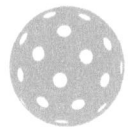

Navigating Conflict on the Court

As one friend said, the best way to beat Teri and Raj is to get them arguing.

Conflict in life and on the pickleball court is inevitable. How you resolve it is key. There will be missed shots, weak dinks, foot faults, etc. Despite being on the same team, the spectrum of reaction is vast. From smiling pretty with gritted teeth to a full on paddle-throwing battle royal.

*"Hey honey? Pass me the popcorn.
This is about to get good."*

Another popular option among couples is to serve up a useless comment with a thick layer of contempt.

"How did you not see that ball going out?"

"Did you just seriously step in the kitchen?"

"Umm, pretty sure that was your forehand!"

One way Teri helps her executive coaching clients know when they're being contemptuous is by paying attention to tone. If the tone you're using can be punctuated with the word *dumbass*, well, that's contempt.

"How did you not see that ball going out... dumbass?"

"Did you seriously just step into the kitchen... dumbass?"

"Umm, pretty sure that was your forehand... dumbass!"

Effective? Absolutely, if you are trying to make your partner feel like shit. Great job. You get the point (but you'll lose the point on the court). Relationship experts Julie and John Gottman say how you fight determines whether you stay together as a couple.[3]

The best option to navigate conflict is to take a deep breath and reset yourself. Then help your partner recover by offering something positive, something supportive, or nothing at

---

3. Jule and John Gottman, Fight Right, Harmony Publishing, Jan. 2024

all. Then move on. Quickly! So you can get ready for the next point. Pickleball is a game of finesse and teamwork.

Who Benefits From Your Fighting?

Your opponent. When you're fighting on the pickleball court, you're definitely giving your opponents the advantage. They'll thank you with a win.

As Stormy says, "I don't mind when my opponents fight because I am fairly certain Steve and I are about to win the next point or two." Strategy!

There will be pressure on the court. It is part of every sport including pickleball. It's also likely one of the reasons you keep coming back again and again. Pressure is addictive. It feels good to have a little competition in life, and pickleball doses up just the right amount.

But how do you respond to pressure? Do you rise or falter? How about your partner?

Don't Make Decisions When You're Pissed

It is never advisable to make decisions when you are angry, irritated, stressed, or low on sleep. Ideally we make decisions when we are grounded and calm. This applies to life and to the pickleball court. Sometimes the mental struggle required to stay magnanimous (and married) feels insurmountable. Sometimes you have to decide if playing together is worth it.

This is why, in times of high intensity and emotion, it's best to take a pause. This is called the power of the pause and it works. Spontaneous decisions in such circumstances never lead to good outcomes.

The Power of an Apology

Pickleball is one of the strangest sports in that "sorry" must be the most common word heard on the court. In no other sport is there a constant stream of "sorries" for hitting a great shot, hitting a ball at your opponent's feet, serving an unreturnable backhand, hitting a ball so that it crawls over the net and drops on your opponent's side. For all these great shots, sorries are given out like candy. Yet, put us in play with our life partners, and it seems those apologies go out the window.

We all act like idiots sometimes because we are messy humans. So when (not if) you break the first rule of pickleball and act like a dick, apologize! Then move on.

> ### Keys To a Real Apology
>
> » Say "I am sorry" and then STOP talking. If your "sorry" is followed by a "but" you've negated or even contradicted yourself. This is not an apology!
>
> » Don't say "I am sorry that you are hurt" because that's about blaming and not taking responsibility. This is not an apology!

- » Don't say "I am sorry but you do the same thing." This is not an apology. That's "what about-ism" and it reduces your relationship to a scorecard. Tit for tat, if you will.
- » Acknowledge that you see that you hurt your spouse, and that you will try not to do it again. Then next time, try harder!

Keep Your Eye On the Prize

When you're in tension with your partner, the need to resolve the conflict can feel like it has to happen right now. Although it might feel urgent, it's not. Plus, the likelihood of making it worse is high and resolving it in the moment is low.

A good strategy is to defer. Calmly decide to discuss something later. You'll still feel all the feelings, but you'll end the escalation. That way, you have a better chance at finishing the game.

Or you can let your ego take over. You're pissed, your partner is pissed. You say something, they say something. Everyone on the court is caught up in the awkward energy, desperate for the game to just end. Fun!

These are choices.

Again, that doesn't mean you don't feel your feelings. It just means you don't make your feelings everyone's responsibility.

Keep your eye on the prize . . . to have fun, play well, and win games. The real prize, however, is always your relationship. It is NEVER worth letting the game negatively impact your relationship on or off the court. Keep that in perspective. It's only pickleball after all.

Use Your Words, Just Not All of Them

We've all said things on the court that we wished we hadn't. Sometimes humans say stupid shit or words we didn't mean, but can never take back. Those words can leave marks, and like Stormy used to tell her son, "Words are like toothpaste. You can't put them back in the tube."

Words like "This is why we should *never* play together" or "What is wrong with you?" Or "Do you even want to get better?" are definitely not going back in the tube. All entwined with an oversized dose of contempt.

Another tip is to avoid superlatives like "always" and "never." It is unlikely that your partner ALWAYS hits the ball out, or NEVER hits the ball over the net, or ALWAYS misses the overhead putaway. Can you hear yourself? While those words might feel true in the moment, we all know they are actually not true.

Superlatives are lazy. They're the words kids use to express hurt. You NEVER let me have fun! You ALWAYS make me clean my room! Take a pause. Say what you mean. It will help your partner hear you and is your best bet for a productive conversation.

Pickleball Divorce is Real

Even with all these communication strategies and conflict resolution tactics, sometimes playing pickleball with your spouse is not the best choice for your relationship. While we wrote this book to help you avoid a "pickleball divorce," we also wanted to acknowledge that sometimes choosing not to play together is the best way to stay together.

Try a Separation First

While pickleball is just a game, sometimes, the best choice is a separation. There's no shame in taking a break from each other. Who knows, you might even find your way back to being on the court together.

There was a time when Teri faced that decision. There has been a moment or 12, when after playing particularly bad pickleball with Raj and his shit attitude, she couldn't take the intensity anymore. They didn't talk for two days and during that time, she wondered - do I even want to be married to this guy?

In their years of marriage, that had never been in question. But the play had become so intense and competitive that the fun was gone. Sadly, to stay married, they agreed they would no longer play together. Even casual, rec play was off limits.

They left for Costa Rica for their annual three-month stay, and found their way back. They'd frequently drill, and they both improved their communication skills not to mention their ability to give and receive feedback. Teri was calmer and less defensive. Raj was kinder in his delivery and open to hearing Teri set boundaries. Eventually, they started to play together again.

The Reality of a Pickleball Divorce

But when you've considered all angles, and it's still too challenging to play together, a pickleball divorce may be the best option. Yes, it's sad. No, it's not ideal. When Teri considered a pickleball divorce, she felt devastated. "We're two smart and successful adults. Why can't we figure out our shit on the pickleball court?!" It seemed so simple.

Yes, sometimes no matter how hard you try, the dynamics just don't work on the court. And a pickleball divorce becomes the best option to keep your marriage together. It can be a "for now" solution, maybe not "forever."

The worst place to decide on a pickleball divorce is on the court during a game. We DO NOT recommend making this decision when you are irked and irritated from your partner's latest tantrum. In pickleball and in life, good choices are best made when you're grounded. Take it off the court and calmly share with your partner how the things they do or say don't work for you. This is a solid starting point for changing the dynamics.

NAVIGATING CONFLICT ON THE COURT

Coming Back to the Court
Asha & Bill

Bill and I were struggling to play pickleball together due to our different playing styles and personalities. After a series of arguments, we decided to take a break.

We started playing mixed doubles with other partners, which was fun, but unsatisfying. After a year, we decided to give it another try. When we returned to the court, we focused on the positive aspects of our partnership and learned to manage our emotions. We discovered that our different playing styles could actually complement each other.

With practice and communication, we were able to overcome our challenges and improve our game. Our pickleball partnership became a source of joy and connection, proving that even the most unlikely partnerships can succeed with effort and understanding.

- Asha

Jed is Our Throuple

One alternative is to play with someone else's husband or wife. Yep! It's just true.

When Raj and Teri were struggling on the court together, it became messy and mean. And since you can't compartmentalize pickleball, they realized that if they wanted to stay together, they couldn't play together. At least not then.

Their friend Jed became their "throuple." For those of you who aren't in the know on this, a throuple is a romantic relationship between three people. While Teri and Raj don't practice this romantically, it was the perfect solution for them on the pickleball court. Jed and Teri played mixed doubles in tournaments, and Raj and Jed played men's doubles together. And it worked. Who knew they would find the perfect partner for both of them, and it wasn't each other!

Fast forward to today. Raj and Teri have found their way back to playing together. But they stick to the rule that they bring in their throuple to avoid playing high-stakes tournaments.

Finding a throuple isn't for everyone. Many couples we know have decided to end it, and just no longer play pickleball together. Not only is it sad, but it also introduces a whole slew of issues.

Who will you play with now?

Will you be okay if your spouse plays with someone else?

Will they be okay with you doing the same?

How will you navigate new partner dynamics?

It's a decision that requires serious consideration, and just like in a relationship, the grass isn't always greener.

Tips for Consciously Choosing a Pickleball Divorce

» Avoid making the decision when you're pissed about your spouse's behavior on the court.

» Consider taking a "for now" break, but not forever.

» Consider how it would feel if your spouse played mixed doubles with another person. Jealous? Just fine? Be honest.

» Keep it about pickleball. Just because you choose not to play pickleball together does not mean you can't navigate life together. Your relationship is ALWAYS the priority (superlative acceptable).

9 Relationship Pitfalls on the Court

1. Blaming your partner: "You should have had that." That was "Yours!"

2. Eye rolls.

3. Audible huffs of frustration.

4. Finger pointing: You are the worst player! You're never going to get better.

5. Ignoring your partner's paddle boops between points.
6. Throwing your paddle.
7. Yelling at your partner.
8. Not apologizing for hitting your partner with the ball.
9. Showing bad sportsmanship (not offering an end of game paddle tap).

KEY TAKEAWAYS

Pickleball Points

- No Fight Club. Conflict is inevitable. Fighting is optional.
- Sorry, not sorry. Make real apologies or don't make them at all.
- Save pickleball divorce as a last resort. Remember, it is you and your partner against the challenge, and not against each other!

Court Chemistry

- What's one action each of you can change today to reduce the on-the-court conflict?

6

How to Elevate Your Pickleball EQ

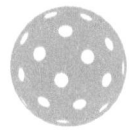

How to Elevate Your Pickleball EQ

"That guy" (hopefully, not your partner) makes an off-color joke. "Read the room," you mutter. That requires emotional intelligence (EQ), and he doesn't have it! Pickleball is no different. Reading your partner on the court is the best way to avoid a battleground of fits and frustration, and questionable life choices.

Why Emotional Intelligence Matters

In the last chapter, we laid out how conflict causes cracks in your relationship. Now, let's fix them!

We typically know when we're being our pleasant, joyous selves, and we mostly demonstrate it when we're playing with our friends and even strangers. You've seen the memes. We are friendly and forgiving: "Bad luck," we claim in an attempt to excuse our friend's terrible shot. "Next time," we say, with hopeful encouragement. But when we play with our partners, the same friendliness and niceties go straight to hell.

Condemnation. "What was that!" Accusations. "That was going out!" No grace is given to the person we are sleeping with. Instead, we hold each other to the highest standards, which are unmeetable, unreasonable and irrational. Failure waiting to happen.

Do You Have Pickleball Emotional Intelligence (EQ)?

When we step onto the court with our spouse, we may have every intention to play our best, rock the fundamentals, and have a great time playing together. Yet, in less than three seconds, after the first ball is served, we devolve into finger-pointing, griping, not-fun-to-play-with jerks. What the heck happens?

HOW TO ELEVATE YOUR PICKLEBALL EQ

Here's the thing. You may be the smartest player on the court, but if you lack awareness, humility and self-control, you are NOT fun to play with. And your lack of Pickleball EQ is glaring!

IQ is your intelligence quotient that measures your cognitive capacity and includes things like logic, reasoning, and problem-solving. Being smart on the court is definitely an advantage, when it comes to outplaying your opponent.

EQ is your emotional intelligence – your self-awareness, self-control, motivation, empathy and social skills. You can imagine, both IQ and EQ are important in successfully navigating the game of pickleball, let alone the game of life. But if you're wondering which one matters more for mastering the court with your spouse? It is EQ for sure.

To navigate the dynamics of your duo, focus on elevating your individual and partnership Pickleball EQ.

Pickleball EQ Quiz

Rate yourself on a scale from 0-5 in each of the following questions:

1. **Do you have court awareness?**

    0 = You have no idea where you are or should be on the court let alone where your partner is

    3 = Most of the time in a point you know where you are and where you should be

    5 = You are almost always in the right spot on the court or working your way there

2. **Are you mentally tough?**

    0 = You are distractible like a golden retriever (squirrel!)

    3 = You are focused and can move on from an error more often than not

    5 = You are a mental force to be reckoned with

3. **Do you have good shot selection and a variety of shots in your arsenal?**

    0 = I only have one shot that I typically use

    3 = I usually know what shot I should hit whether I can hit it or not

    5 = I am a shot ninja and know exactly the right one to use

4. **Do you have good partner communication?**

    0 = I am supposed to communicate with my partner?

3 = We communicate well most of the time

5 = We could host our own podcast, we are so in sync

5. **Do you know the platinum rule?**

    0 = What rule?

    3 = I know it but it goes out the window when my partner is a dick

    5 = I abide by this platinum nugget in life and pickleball

6. **Can you be a goldfish?**

    0 = I don't even know what this means

    3 = Sometimes it is hard for me to move on from an error - mine or theirs

    5 = I'm a goldfish expert and am already on to the next point

Now tally up your total number of points.

24-30 points = You are a Pickleball EQ dream and a great partner to play with.

18-24 points = You have good Pickleball EQ with some room to improve.

12-18 points = Hmmm. You can do better.

0-12 points = Have you considered pickleball singles?

** This quiz is not scientifically validated but you get the gist.

A True Test
Mackenzie

I'm not kidding when I say pickleball is testing my 8-year marriage. We both love the game, but now that my husband and I are playing together, we are at each other's throats. It's crazy!

With the amount of pressure we put on each other, you'd think we were being scouted for the PPA. We are not! But we act as if our lives depend on every next point.

We've never had the need to go to marriage counseling, or experienced this in any other aspect of our lives. And yet, we love playing and want to play together. Does anyone have a good pickleball therapist?

- Mackenzie

As the Abba song says, "*Knowing me, knowing you (a ha). There is nothing we can do.*"

Oh wait.. that's a break-up song. No irony here.

Well, the good news is, you can dial up your Pickleball EQ and make the experience of playing pickleball with your significant other fun. It starts with knowing me and knowing you. By the way, this is a good section to read out loud to your partner.

Court Awareness

Knowing Me: Ask yourself, what sort of headspace am I in? Am I anxious or angry? Delighted or excited? How can I get grounded so I can stay focused on the game?

Knowing You: This is all about your awareness of your partner: What sort of headspace is your spouse in? Since you can't read your lover's mind (nope . . . You can't!), why not take a moment and check in with them before the game starts? Share a bit about how you're feeling too.

This kind of clarity is bonding and is a gamechanger for smoother vibes on the court. It also helps you learn as a couple how to check in with each other in other areas of your life.

Mental Toughness

It is frustrating as a partner to run for all the tough shots, get them back over the net, and nail that fabulous ATP[4]... only to have your partner casually hit the ball straight into the net.

We have been on both sides of that play and it sucks! You're almost asking for a kitchen knife moment. However, if you want to salvage the game and perk up the vibe, then dial up your self-control.

Yes, you will naturally want to criticize, finger point, and declare your disgruntlement with a thunderous eye roll. But what

---

4. An ATP shot, or Around the Post shot, is a pickleball shot that's hit from outside the sidelines, around the net post, and into the opponent's court.

if you didn't? What if you restrained yourself from saying something mean? What if you used that mythological self-control everyone talks about?

You can. Even when you think your partner is breaking the first rule of pickleball and being the dick, resist the urge to join them. Stay high, when they go low.

Get Platinum

One more rule to abide by, the third rule of pickleball, if you will, is the Platinum Rule. While the Golden Rule is much more widely known and is about treating others in the way YOU want to be treated, The Platinum Rule is much more impactful for the pickleball court.

Dave Kerpen, author of the book *The Art of People*, coined the term and defines the rule as 'do unto others as THEY would want done to them.' Everyone is different so if we treat them how we want to be treated, that might not fly. Instead, treat your spouse the way they want to be treated on the court and watch what happens.

On the drive to the courts, you're excited. You get to do something fun with your partner, your person, who happens to be the last person you'd ever want to hurt. So get Platinum. Find your self-control and don't be a dick.

Be A Goldfish

Take a page out of Ted Lasso's playbook. According to Ted, a goldfish only has a three-second memory span. When he tells his team to be a goldfish, he's telling them to "forget about it." Move on.

This is an important lesson for all of us, especially the over-achievers. We tend to be hard on ourselves, which frequently translates into being hard on our partner too. Dwelling on the mistakes of the past keeps you squarely in the past. Sure, learn from the mistake. Play better. And MOVE ON!

Empathize

Couples with shared interests like each other more and feel greater understanding and empathy for each other.

How you react when your partner drives a shot into the net or swings for the rafters and hits one long is a choice. Offering your spouse support and encouragement goes much farther than slinging f-bombs!

Here's another opportunity to invoke the third rule of pickleball. Be Platinum. Treat your partner how they want to be treated when they make a mistake. We all make mistakes so don't be a dick about it.

Understand that if your partner's doing the best they can, in the situation they're in, do you really want to make them feel bad by taking out your frustration on them? Just 20 minutes ago, they were your person.

If you want to elevate your Pickleball IQ, then do that, but not at the expense of your Pickleball EQ and never at the expense of the relationship. Pickleball IQ and strategy can be worked on individually or as a couple. It will help you decide what shots to take, how to be strategic, and how to move together on the court.

But none of it will matter without Pickleball EQ because you or your spouse storming off the court or vowing never to play together again is never a path to a happy ending.

Opposites Attract
Patty & Zach

On the court, Zach and I were like oil and water – constantly clashing. He's the laid-back free spirit, always cracking jokes and chatting with other players. I'm the highly competitive Type A personality, always striving for perfection.

On the court, I couldn't stand his casual attitude, and he couldn't handle my criticism. We argued constantly, and our performance suffered.

After a particularly embarrassing loss, we had a serious talk. We realized that our differences, while challenging, could also be our greatest strength. My competitive drive could push us to practice harder, and his laid-back attitude could help us stay relaxed and enjoy the game.

We established our own golden rule: only positive talk on the court. We agreed to support each other, celebrate our successes, and learn from our mistakes.

Wow! My competitive spirit was tempered by his positive attitude, and his laid-back demeanor was energized by my drive. We became a formidable team, winning several tournaments and earning a reputation as the "Pickleball Odd Couple."

- Patty

KEY TAKEAWAYS

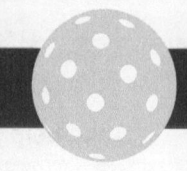

Pickleball Points

- Read the room (and the court): Awareness is key to avoiding pickleball pitfalls.
- Master your mind, master the court. Increase your mental toughness.
- The Platinum Rule: Treat your spouse the way they want to be treated on the court.
- Be a goldfish. Let that shit go.

Court Chemistry

- Of all the aspects of Pickleball EQ: court awareness, mental toughness, demonstrating the Platinum Rule, being a goldfish and showing empathy…which one do each of you want to improve on to advance your pickleball game and your partnership?

7
Your Pickleball Love Language

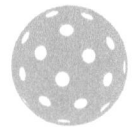

Your Pickleball Love Language

Let's be real: Nothing tests a relationship quite like a game of pickleball. You show up intending to slay the court together. Joking. Booping. All of a sudden, you're up in your partner's business about their dreadful dinking skills. They match your vigor with a spray of obscenities.

Is it a pickleball court or a cage match? Hard to tell.

IN A PICKLE

Pickleball pro and Stormy's camp instructor Kevin Beeson says, "Your only role in pickleball doubles is to make your partner look good."

Wow. It sounds so easy when he says it.

A few years back, Gary Chapman wrote The Five Love Languages, a popular book that helped many couples learn to understand each other and validate how different two people are in one relationship.

> **The Love Languages**
>
> 1. Acts of Service
>
> 2. Quality Time
>
> 3. Words of Affirmation
>
> 4. Physical Touch
>
> 5. Receiving Gifts

Knowing your partner's love language cracks a code in a way that allows each of you to feel heard, appreciated and understood. While Teri is a huge fan of all things witchy, she dismissed the Love Languages as a double dose of self-help bullshit. Then, she figured out she was wrong.

Instead of talking past each other or simply pissing each other off, this hyper-data based approach helps couples all over the world minimize their conflict and appreciate each other's differences.

That's an advantage in any relationship!

And of course, we've translated this into pickleball speak, to help you increase the chances of a solid partnership on and off the court.

Stormy's and Steve's love language is Physical Touch. Those high fives, paddle boops, or pats on the bottom make them feel in sync and motivate them to both play great. Their go-to before, during, and after a game is to offer up a sweaty hug.

Not so much for Teri and Raj. Teri's love language is Words of Affirmation. The more Raj encourages her with words from his heart, the better she plays. Similarly (but different), Raj's love language is Quality Time. He appreciates phone-down, uninterrupted time with Teri. That means the more she stays focused and fully present on the pickleball court, the more Raj feels loved. A true test is whether she gets the score right.

Since there are two individuals on your side of the court with different skills, different games, and different mindsets, the challenge is to bridge the gap by leveraging each other's strengths and minimizing each other's weaknesses.

Knowing these little secrets about each other helps. Relationships are complex, but playing pickleball together doesn't need to overly complicate them. The best way to think about playing together is to hit a great shot that sets your partner up for the perfect put-away. Shake and bake, baby! That's a winning strategy.

If you don't know your love language, then Google it, and take one of the many free quizzes. Even better, do it together. That's what we did, and it makes for a great date night.

Pickleball Love Language Cheat Sheet:

Acts of Service – Actions speak louder than words if this is your partner's love language.

- Book the court.
- Fill their water bottle and pack snacks.
- Help with the honey-do list so the two of you can get out on the court together.
- Book a lesson from the local pro for your partner.
- Take the lobs so your partner doesn't have to.

Quality Time – Quality is the key word. It's about being attentive and focused, which will make your partner feel loved. Because there's no such thing as a bad day on the pickleball court.

- Set aside focused time to practice and drill together.
- Set up a regular game with another couple whom you both enjoy.
- Join a club together.
- Play a round robin together.
- Video your game and analyze it together.

Words of Affirmation – Words of encouragement, understanding, and appreciation will make your partner feel deeply valued and connected. You can't go wrong with positive encouragement and that will be their jam!

- "You got this!"
- "Great get!"
- "Damn baby! Where did that serve come from!"
- "Great try!"
- "I like that idea."

Physical Touch – Love is generally best communicated in the form of physical affection, such as holding hands, hugging.

- High-fives.
- Consensual butt pats.
- Paddle boops no matter what happened in the point.
- Chest bumps.
- More hugs.

Receiving Gifts – Big gifts or small trinkets that show you know your partner well makes them feel loved.

- "Let's get you a new paddle."
- "I bought you a new pair of pickleball shoes."
- Give a pickleball care package: socks, towel, wristband, new balls.
- Gift a lesson with a pro they like.
- Surprise them with a pickleball outfit they would rock the court in.

That's What I Meant

Understanding each other's love language helps avoid the oh-so-common mistake of what you said versus what you *meant*. Take the following, as an example.

Stormy and Steve were playing in a high stakes tournament in Utah. The air was hot, and their competition was good. They found themselves at a standoff. It was a match point and the tension between teams was at its peak.

They served. Steve returned.

And then their opponent hit a perfect drop just over the net. Stormy hauled her ass to the kitchen to get her paddle under it, while her man gruffly yelled "you must do something with that ball!"

WTF! As if I had some other idea, she screamed in her head.

Then, as if in slow motion, she tensed her hand, tightened her grip, and the ball ricocheted directly off her paddle into the net. Game over.

They made their way to the net and graciously congratulated their opponents. As Stormy turned away from them, her smile turned to rage. She seethingly said to Steve

"Never! Do! That! Again!"

After a few minutes Stormy calmed down and decided the best course of action was to share what would have worked better for her. She told him that had he said something like "go baby go" or "you got this" she would have sprang into action with his encouragement feeding the wind beneath her pickleball skirt.

He looked at her squarely and said: "Well, that's what I meant."

Oy vey! This was a classic example where "what you said and what you meant" were not even remotely close. Make it easy on everyone and say what you mean and mean what you say. Knowing your partner's love language will help in this effort and perhaps change what you say and what you do to be more in line with what your partner needs.

Bonus Tip - Flirt!

Why not use the pickleball court to up your flirting game with your spouse? Yeah, flirting! Remember that thing you did when you were first dating and would muse over how to seduce, entice, and enthrall each other?

It's easy to get caught up adulting, where fun and playfulness are the lowest priorities. The pickleball court can be a great terrain to bring sexy back. Compliment your partner on the court, give them an inviting wink, or admire their tenacity running for that lob over your shoulder.

We know this is a gamechanger, because we saw it in action. Teri and Raj were full of giggles one day at rec play, and Stormy finally realized what was going on. As Raj admired and shared with Teri how adorable she was, running all over the court for balls that were in fact going out. He turned a feedback moment into a flirting moment. Way to go, Raj!

Love Language Tips To Improve Your Game

» Say what you mean and mean what you say.

» Know your partner's love language and how it translates into what you do and say on the pickleball court.

» Remember, it's the two of you against your opponent, the ball, and the net. Not the two of you against each other.

KEY TAKEAWAYS

Pickleball Points

The 5 love languages as they relate to pickleball:

- Words of Affirmation - "Great job babe"
- Quality Time - "Let's go drill, just the two of us"
- Acts of Service - "I did the laundry so we can go play"
- Physical Touch - That extra paddle boop after a lost point
- Receiving Gifts - "Got you the brand new Vulcan ball"

Court Chemistry

- 💜 Identify your and your partner's love language. What is one thing each of you can change to better communicate with your partner in their love language?

8

A Banger and a Dinker Walk Into a Bar

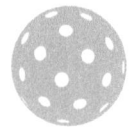

A Banger and a Dinker Walk Into a Bar

One of the things Raj says is to be "Opposite George." If your man is of the age where he knows all the lines from Seinfeld, then he'll know exactly what that means. Admittedly, we've found this to be a not-too-terrible strategy.

In layman's terms, that means do the opposite of what you think you should do. If you never poach, then try it. If you always go for line shots and hit them out, then go for the shot down the middle. You'll hit it in. If you can't resist swinging at balls that are going out, then let them bounce and that way you'll know what to do next.

Opposite Action

In the psych world, we call this strategy Opposite Action. And it is a good one. You know what doing the same thing is going to get you ... more of the same. Einstein said the definition of insanity is doing the same thing and expecting a different result.

It's no wonder that on the pickleball court, so much of what we do can seem insane, making the same mistakes over and over. The whole goal of this book is to play better pickleball with your spouse, so do something different to achieve that goal.

If you're the type who can't resist offering unsolicited or negative feedback, then try a more positive approach. Or say nothing! Less is more on the pickleball court. Or if you hit your third shot drive into the net, change it up! Practice your third shot drops or fifth shot drives. There are always multiple ways to approach change. If you have been slamming all your overheads long or into the net, try a gentler "kiss the baby" shot taking the speed off, and dropping an unreturnable ball into the kitchen.

In other words – if nothing changes, nothing changes.

I Got Your Back

What is your playing style and what is your partner's? Are you a banger, meaning all power and no dinking? Or are you a finesse player and love your soft game? There is no one-size-fits-all in pickleball and there is no perfect combination in partner play. That's why you want to know what you and your partner are good at, and then capitalize.

One of the many beautiful things about this game is that there is always something to work on, a strategy to try, or a new approach to take to play better together. There is always something to learn, which increases the addiction and is one of the reasons why this sport is so damn popular.

The goal is to be balanced in your play and work as a team. A good team moves and relates as a unit. If your partner gets pulled, you cover the middle. If you move up from the baseline, your partner moves too. When you get the opportunity, you squeeze the court together, and make it hard for your opponent to return the shot.

Moving together on the pickleball court is like moving together through life. It's about teamwork and having each other's back.

Give Grace
Eric & Matt

Matt and I have been together for years and playing pickleball together has been an incredible journey. At first, our

> competitive spirits lead to a lot of angst. But we realized we needed to change our approach and learn how to give each other grace and be more forgiving. It didn't happen overnight, but it's been a gamechanger for our partnership.
>
> Now, playing pickleball together is more than just a sport. It's a way for us to connect, have fun, and challenge ourselves. We've made lifelong friends through the pickleball community and we're so grateful for the experiences we've shared.
>
> - Eric

You Share Neurochemistry and Physiology

As a team playing on a very small court, the two of you will actually share moods. Science has proven that we share moods with our spouses. That means if your partner comes onto the court joyful and positive, they can quickly elevate you to feel the same. Who doesn't want that? Exercise, like sex, releases endorphins and they definitely do a body and mind good.

But if either of you comes onto the court sulking and nasty, the mood can devolve quickly, and so will your game. The key is to be aware of the mood you bring onto the court. This is not to say that you have to be "happy-go-lucky" all the time, but know that your mood impacts your partner, your play, and theirs too.

And, beyond mood, you also share these health benefits together:

1. **Healthy Lifestyle**

    We all know couples where one person is fit and the other is, we'll say, less fit. But even at different levels, staying active together is a great way to have fun and navigate aging. Your 80-year-old self will thank you, since pickleball is an activity you can play at any age.

2. **Fitness**

    Pickleball is a total-body workout. It boosts flexibility, speeds up reaction times, sharpens hand-eye coordination, and engages your brain, as you grapple with the quirky scoring system.

3. **Calorie Burning**

    One hour of pickleball singles is equal to playing tennis for two hours. While doubles may be half the calories but twice the fun (allegedly), playing pickleball is what matters. The bursts of stops and starts use fast-twitch muscle fibers, and as we age, we tend to use those less and less. Playing pickleball burns 8-10 calories per minute, and those minutes add up quickly.

4. **Stress Relief**

    Pickleball won't solve all your problems, and on some days it will undoubtedly create new ones. If you're willing to "just have fun" and not take it too seriously, it's a great way to blow off steam. We can all agree that even a challenging day is a great day when it's on the pickleball court, and we can all benefit from lowering our stress.

All this tracks back to the importance of communication and Pickleball EQ. When you let your partner know it's a rough day or you're feeling low energy, maybe they can take a ball or two to compensate. Imagine how having that awareness positions you both for success. We don't play pickleball in a vacuum, so your mood impacts both you and your partner. That's why it's important to be aware and communicate.

Leave it on the Court

Your bad day can't ruin it for everyone else. Remember, it's just pickleball. It's supposed to be playful and fun. When you're trying to get better, it can be hard at times. But don't let what happens on the pickleball court ruin the rest of your day or your relationship.

If it ceases to be fun, then that is on you. Don't make it about your significant other.

There are times when Teri feels Raj is an open spout of constant criticism. If you asked him, she's sure he'd say it's all constructive. He knows she wants to get better so in his mind he's being helpful, and it does start out that way.

But predictably, it sinks into what feels like Captain Obvious mansplaining every mistake. "You're swinging," "You're stabbing," "That ball was out by a mile," "That dink was weak." And on and on . . . and on.

Finally, when they are both sufficiently frustrated, he throws up his hands.

"I give up! You're not coachable!"

"Are you fucking kidding me?! I am a coach!" she shoots back.

Then the game is over. The earth rights itself on its axis, and they both get into the car and discuss what they want for dinner. Grace!

KEY TAKEAWAYS

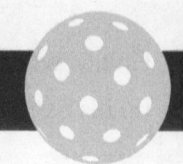

Pickleball Points

- Change your game to change the game.
- Your mood is contagious. Spread positivity on the court.
- No carnage: Leave it on the court.

Court Chemistry

- ♥ What can each of you do, or not do, to increase trust and show you've got each other's back?

9
Safe Words & Other Success Strategies

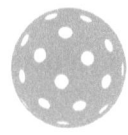

Safe Words & Other Success Strategies

Pickleball strategy is as much about safe words as it is about setting up the winning point. While mastering the dink is essential, true champions know the importance of a power shot down the middle, followed by a well-placed chide, "Who's got the middle?"

If you can answer YES (or mostly yes) to both of the following questions, you are winning.

1. Are you having fun playing together?

2. Are you avoiding being dicks to each other?

If you can't say yes just yet, then let's talk strategy.

Safe Words

We love safe words. No one ever wants to find themselves in a compromised position against their will. Why should pickleball be any different? Sure, you might not be physically bound, but you can justifiably feel emotionally contorted to the degree that it just needs to stop!

When the heat rises and the tension builds, it is hard to hear any kind of direction, feedback or command your partner is giving you. If you're making mistakes, *you know* you're making mistakes. If for some ungodly reason your partner chooses that exact moment to let you know *they also know* you're making mistakes, then too bad for them for using terrible judgment.

This can go multiple ways, and for most humans, it never ends well. Unless you safeguard your relationship by taking a page out of the BDSM[5] playbook and start using safe words.

---

5. BDSM is a variety of often erotic practices or roleplaying involving bondage, discipline, dominance and submission, sadomasochism, and other related interpersonal dynamics. Don't Google this unless you want all sorts of risque things coming up in your search.

SAFE WORDS & OTHER SUCCESS STRATEGIES

Before you start the game, agree to a safe word. That way when you are flooded with frustration, and somehow your partner thinks it's a coachable moment, you sound the alarm to let them know they couldn't be more wrong!

PUMPERNICKEL is Teri and Raj's safe word at parties, picnics, and on the pickleball court. Instead of reacting with "Shut the fuck up!" she says "Where is the pumpernickel? Do we have any pumpernickel?" But she doesn't say "Stop being a fucking pumpernickel."

Saying that last one would be a misuse of the safe word. It's an exacerbation. So instead, the blood seeps from her lips having bitten her tongue to keep from saying anything she can't take back.

PINEAPPLE is Stormy and Steve's safe word both on and off the pickleball court. When Steve offers unsolicited advice, let's say during a point, rather than unleashing on him, Stormy simply looks at him directly and says "PINEAPPLE," which is his cue to zip it.

For the novices in the room, a safe word is an agreed-to word between you and your partner that, once said, leaves no ambiguity in what happens next, namely FULL STOP! Don't say another word! If you want to win more points, then having a safe word is a foolproof strategy.

> **Here are a few samples:**
>
> **Good safe words:** Cottonball, Squishy, Kumquat
>
> **Bad safe words:** Pickle (too confusing), Kerfuffle (kind of a mouthful), Fuck off (defeats the purpose)

Before you play another game, choose your pickleball safe word. Then, try it out on the court.

Psychological Warfare

As it's said, all is fair in love and war. And why shouldn't the same be true for pickleball? Psychological warfare is essentially the art of using mental tactics to gain a competitive advantage over your opponents. Sure, being great players is how you close the deal, but mind games that influence your opponents' emotions and disrupt their focus are fair game.

For example:

- **Body language and intimidation:** Using strong, confident body language can make opponents feel less confident. Conversely, as we've mentioned, your frustration or tension on the court gives your opponents an advantage.

- **Shot selection and placement:** Deliberately placing shots in specific locations can disrupt your opponents' rhythm and force errors.

- **Pace of play:** Controlling the pace of the game can throw off your opponents' timing and decision-making. Patience is key!

- **Verbal cues and distractions:** Strategic use of verbal cues, such as grunts or exclamations, can be distracting. Teri and Raj yell random words throughout a game – "sneaker," "poacher," "crawler." So much so that their opponents start using the same words to describe shots.

- **Shit-Talkers:** Others use shit-talking to intimidate their opponents. But we've found that it's usually the shit-talkers who have nothing to back it up!

Ultimately, psychological warfare is about understanding your opponents, knowing your own strengths and weaknesses, and using that knowledge to gain a mental edge. It's a subtle form of competition that can make a significant difference in the outcome of a match.

Winning Strategies

Here are a few more strategies. If you're not good at them, consider this your practice list.

Disciplined Dinkery

This requires patience, precision, and a lot of practice. If you and your partner can be disciplined dinkers, you can own your opponents. Especially if they're bangers.

Who's Got the Middle

When your opponents are guarding the lines, the best shot you or your partner can hit is straight down the middle. Chaos will ensue as your opponents rush to the middle, clanking paddles in a pulsating frenzy to return the ball.

Don't Start Something You Can't Finish

Again, "patience you must have." You dink. They dink. You dink. They dink, but the ball pops up. You drive. They return the shot. A firefight ensues! If you started it, be certain you and your partner can finish it and win the point.

Help Your Partner

When your partner is in trouble, help them! If a shot pulls them off the court, you cover the middle. After they've served and are trying to get to the kitchen, help them by poaching the ball. Buy them some time so they can get into position.

Target Weakness

One of your opponents is weaker than the other. Figure out which one, and then make sure you and your partner are hitting the ball to them. If they're both excellent, aim for shots to their backhand. Unless you're playing Anna Leigh Waters, most players have a weaker backhand.

Get to the Kitchen

In doubles with your lover, the key is to BOTH get to the kitchen. Just like in life, being divided on the court is rarely a winning strategy. So be aware of where your partner is, move as a unit, and BOTH work your way to the kitchen as soon as you can. As Raj says, "Good things happen when you're both at the kitchen, because that's where the game of pickleball is played . . . So get there!"

The Ultimate Advantage

It goes without saying, but of course we'll say it: being masterful communicators on the court will give you and your spouse the ultimate advantage. Just watch! When the two of you put all your great skills to work and communicate together throughout the game, you'll see how many games you win. And how in awe of your partnership everyone else will be.

Drill Me!

You don't get better at pickleball from just playing games. You improve your game with drilling and practice. Yes, we said it. PRACTICE. Yet so many couples just hop on the court and play their regular game, hitting balls into the net or out of bounds, and accumulating rolling numbers of unforced errors.

If you only desire to be as good as you are, then rec play is your jam. But if you want to improve your mixed doubles game, it is wise for you and your partner to practice. It is also a great place to practice all the communication and relationship tips in this book and start to play better as a team on the court, and in life.

Smoothed Edges
Lori & Ben

I love my husband, but sometimes on the pickleball court, I seriously have to remind myself of that.

We are both competitive, but Ben is the more aggressive player, always looking for the perfect shot. I, on the other hand, am more meticulous, focusing on precision and strategy. You'd think this would be complementary, but more often than not, it leads to fights.

Despite our frequent disagreements, we can't deny our chemistry on the court. When we're playing well, we're a force! But our competitive nature often overshadows our teamwork.

We realized that our constant bickering was not only hindering our performance on the court, but also harming our relationship. We decided to hire a coach to help us channel our competitive energy in a more positive direction.

When we returned to the court, we came with a new perspective. We are a work in progress, but agree we've smoothed out the sharp edges, making us better partners on and off the court.

- Lori

Celebrate Each Other

One of the best aspirations for pickleball is that the game you play is consistent. But the reality is some days you think you are ready to go amateur-pro and the very next day you feel like you've never played before.

The ups and downs in your game are in fact part of the game. Which is why it is vitally important to celebrate your own victories, your spouse's victories, and your relationship victories on the court.

And by victories we are not necessarily referring to the winning of points or matches. We are talking about the little wins like successfully dropping that third shot, getting to the kitchen with a split step, putting away that overhead smash, etc.

Small wins are wins. Celebrate them. The more you focus on the small stuff, the more your game will improve, and the more fun you'll have.

Finally, this might be the most powerful success strategy of all. Keep it all in perspective. It's pickleball for God's sake. It's something that's fun to do together, keeps you fit and gives your brain a good workout.

If you're new to the game and playing with your partner, or trying to get back to a good place with your spouse, then be patient. You'll get there. The game is meant to be playful, fast, strategic, and addictive – all the makings of a great time spent together.

Tips for Success

» Have a calm conversation with your partner about what works and what doesn't in the dynamic between the two of you on the court.

» Keep it about the pickleball court. Don't bring up something your partner did or said years ago after too many drinks at your cousin's wedding.

» Notice how YOU are with your partner and not just how they are with you. Both communication and conflict take two people.

» Practice and drill together to up-level your game. Practice the shots that are most challenging and find new ways to be in relationship on the court.

» Don't be a dick.

» Choose and use a safe word.

» Celebrate each other's small wins.

» Be willing to make a real apology.

» Remember to have fun. It's the point of the game.

» Practice gratitude that the two of you are playing a sport together and having fun.

KEY TAKEAWAYS

Pickleball Points

- Don't just play the game, understand it: Strategy beats brute force.
- Master the dink, dominate the game. Patience is power.
- Practice makes progress. Get better, have more fun.
- Small wins, big smiles. Celebrate every victory.

Court Chemistry

- What is the safe word you both agree to, and what exactly do you both agree to do or stop doing when the safe word is spoken?
- As a team, what do you both want to be known for? And what strategies do you both need to work on to make it so?

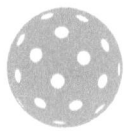

Conclusion

Couples who play together stay together. Let pickleball make you a stronger couple.

In parting, two of the most incredible benefits of pickleball are friendship and community. Pickleball is more than a game. It's a crucible for relationships, a test of character, and a surprising source of personal growth. It is an incredible tool for building friendship both within and outside your partnership, and is a catalyst for connection to a community of cool people.

Makes you wonder how you used to spend your time before this sport took over your life.

But beyond camaraderie, pickleball is a proving ground where skills are honed and confidence soars. When the club closes and the lights turn off, the lessons learned on the pickleball court reverberate far beyond the white lines.

So remember, every point, every match, is an opportunity – a chance to build a stronger, more resilient partnership in love and pickleball.

– Stormy & Teri

CONCLUSION

Stay Connected

We'd love to hear from you. And send us your videos!

www.loveandpickleball.net

@love_and_pickleball

@loveandpickleball

@love.and.pickleball

Stormy@loveandpickleball.net

Teri@loveandpickleball.net

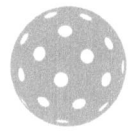

Glossary

Dreambreaker - the fun-to-watch last game between MLP teams for the premier championship.

Fix That Shit - what Paige (a dear friend of ours) yells at her husband when he keeps repeating the same mistake over and over. Or any mistake for that matter.

Heartmaker - when your partner sets you up for a 'shake and bake' and you put away the winning point!

Kitchen Knife Moments - how Renee (a good friend of Teri's) describes those moments when she truly wants to stab her husband. We apply it to pickleball when you wish you had a knife in your hand instead of a paddle.

KYLE! - what we yell when the ball crawls over the net and lands on the other side creating an ungettable shot for the other team (a consistent shot by Kyle Owasaki, a frequent player with Teri and Raj).

Lovetaker - when you set your partner up for a 'shake and bake' and they hit the put-away shot into the net! Aaaargh!

The Party - what pro Kevin Beeson calls the kitchen. And when you and your partner both get there you have an 80% chance of winning the point.

Picklitude - when you get sassy or grumpy from not playing pickleball.

Poacher - taking your partner's shot (You better make it!).

Reacher - standing in a wide stance, while reaching into the kitchen to take the ball on the fly and missing.

Shake & Bake - when one partner of the serving team in doubles pickleball drives the third shot, while the other partner crashes (i.e., runs to) the kitchen and smashes the ball over the net scoring the point.[6]

Stabber - when the ball comes down the middle and your partner lines up their perfect forehand shot, but you stab with your back hand and miss. Unless you are pro player Anna Leigh Waters with a whipping backhand that could kill an elephant, don't be a Stabber!

Who's Got the Middle - a "rally cry" by Dave "the Badger" Weinbach, when your opponent hits the ball straight down the middle and you and your partner look at each other dumbfounded while the ball bounces off the court.

---

6. https://thepickler.com/pickleball-blog/what-is-shake-bake-in-pickleball/

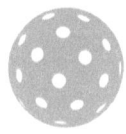

Acknowledgments

While only two authors are listed, the braintrust of this book was immense.

Thank you Renee Womack and Paige Hart for the insights, honesty, and coined phrases for describing the challenges of playing with your husbands. And thank you Jed Miracle. Just thank you.

Thank you Joe Rosenthal, Stormy's stepdad, who brilliantly and easily came up with the name of this book. He doesn't know much about pickleball, but he knows a lot about relationships and love.

Thanks to all our pickleball coaches who have made us better players and taught us to have a blast while improving our game. And to our exquisite pickleball communities that span the globe – from Utah to Texas to Costa Rica and on. We are grateful to be surrounded, challenged and uplifted by such phenomenal humans and players.

And special thanks to Mason Hill, Stormy's son, "for being the light of my life and my greatest teacher in all things love. Being your mom is my greatest honor."

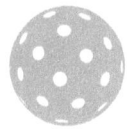

About the Authors

Dr. Stormy Hill

Dr. Stormy Hill, OTR/L, is the owner of two occupational therapy businesses helping special education students and adults with mental health challenges. She is a pioneer in the development of sensory rooms in rehab facilities. Stormy had worked for over 14 years as a mental health occupational therapist and is also a certified intimacy coach, founder of Love Deep Lab, and a national speaker on relationships and wellness.

She has been featured in the NY Post and Thrive Business Magazine For Women, and was elected as one of the Women to Watch in Utah Business Magazine in 2014. She also was a celebrity authority and #1 Amazon best-selling author in The Transformational Journey - Stories on Business, Life and Happiness.

She has a BA from Duke University, her medical doctorate from Michigan State University College of Human Medicine, and her MS in Occupational Therapy from University of Southern California.

For VIP relationship coaching, speaking inquiries, or to learn more visit www.drstormyschiller.com and on @drstormyschiller

Teri Citterman

Known for her direct style, Teri Citterman helps CEOs, senior leaders, and executive teams leverage their power and influence to successfully achieve organizational change.

Teri is the founder and principal of Talonn, a firm that helps good thinkers become great leaders. As a certified executive performance coach, award-winning writer, and author of the book "From the CEO's Perspective," Teri merges her experience in corporate communications and ghostwriting with her knowledge gained from coaching and interviewing hundreds of CEOs.

She has a keen ear for what's not being said and quickly translates insights into action that achieves measurable results. Executives who work with Teri demonstrate greater focus and confidence for scaling their leadership as evidenced by stronger executive presence, decisiveness, and equal footing.

Her clients include fast-paced, high-growth start-ups and complex organizations like Alaska Airlines, DocuSign, University of Washington Medicine, PayPal, Brinks Global Services, Bill & Melinda Gates Investments, Microsoft, and Lockheed Martin.

To learn more about executive coaching, CEO events or ghostwriting, visit www.Talonnllc.com or  @tericitterman

Teri and Stormy on the courts at ACRE Resort, San Jose del Cabo, Mexico

www.ingramcontent.com/pod-product-compliance
Lightning Source LLC
Chambersburg PA
CBHW030446100526
44580CB00001B/5